WEDGES

IN MY
MAKERSPACE

by Tim Miller and
Rebecca Sjonger

CRABTREE
Publishing Company
www.crabtreebooks.com

For Ari, Isaac, Elias, and Zara

Authors: Tim Miller, Rebecca Sjonger

Series research and development:
 Reagan Miller

Editorial director: Kathy Middleton

Editor: Janine Deschenes

Design: Margaret Amy Salter

Proofreader: Petrice Custance

Photo research: Margaret Amy Salter

Production coordinator and prepress technician:
 Margaret Amy Salter

Print coordinator: Margaret Amy Salter

Photographs:

Shutterstock: © AC Rider p 16

Craig Culliford: pp8-9

All other images by Shutterstock

Library and Archives Canada Cataloguing in Publication

Miller, Tim, 1973-, author
        Wedges in my makerspace / Tim Miller, Rebecca Sjonger.

(Simple machines in my makerspace)
Includes index.
Issued in print and electronic formats.
ISBN 978-0-7787-3374-4 (hardcover).--
ISBN 978-0-7787-3382-9 (softcover).--
ISBN 978-1-4271-1904-9 (HTML)

        1. Wedges--Juvenile literature. 2. Makerspaces--Juvenile literature.
I. Sjonger, Rebecca, author II. Title.

TJ1201.W44M55 2017   j621.8   C2016-907450-1
                                                            C2016-907451-X

Library of Congress Cataloging-in-Publication Data

Names: Miller, Tim, 1973- author. | Sjonger, Rebecca, author.
Title: Wedges in my makerspace / Tim Miller and Rebecca Sjonger.
Description: New York, New York : Crabtree Publishing Company, [2017] |
  Series: Simple machines in my makerspace | Audience: Ages 8-11. |
  Audience: Grades 4 to 6. | Includes index.
Identifiers: LCCN 2016054110 (print) | LCCN 2016056160 (ebook) |
  ISBN 9780778733744 (reinforced library binding : alk. paper) |
  ISBN 9780778733829 (pbk. : alk. paper) |
  ISBN 9781427119049 (Electronic HTML)
Subjects: LCSH: Wedges--Juvenile literature. | Simple machines--Juvenile
  literature. | Makerspaces--Juvenile literature.
Classification: LCC TJ1201.W44 M55 2017 (print) | LCC TJ1201.W44 (ebook)
  | DDC 621.8/11--dc23
LC record available at https://lccn.loc.gov/2016054110

Crabtree Publishing Company

www.crabtreebooks.com   1-800-387-7650

Printed in Canada/032017/BF20170111

Published in Canada
Crabtree Publishing
616 Welland Ave.
St. Catharines, Ontario
L2M 5V6

Published in the United States
Crabtree Publishing
PMB 59051
350 Fifth Avenue, 59th Floor
New York, New York 10118

Published in the United Kingdom
Crabtree Publishing
Maritime House
Basin Road North, Hove
BN41 1WR

Published in Australia
Crabtree Publishing
3 Charles Street
Coburg North
VIC 3058

CONTENTS

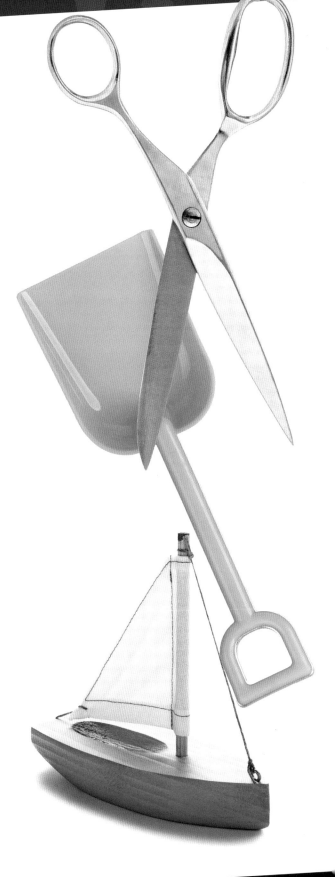

YOU CAN BE A MAKER!

Do you know what it means to be a maker? Makers dream up new ways to do tasks or solve problems. They find new ways to reuse everyday items and try new and exciting experiments. Do you think up creative ideas you can't wait to try? If so, this book is for you! The following projects will inspire your creativity, from creating a boat to finding new ways to finish chores.

TEAMWORK

Makers often team up to share their skills and supplies. Working in a group also leads to more ideas and points of view. This sparks creativity! **Makerspaces** are places where makers work together. Some communities have makerspaces in places such as schools or local libraries. You could also set up your own makerspace and invite some friends to join you!

A new way of learning

There is no right or wrong way to make something.
Makers know that:

✓ The only limit is your imagination.

✓ Every idea or question—even ones that seem silly—
could lead to something amazing.

✓ Each team member adds value to a project.

✓ Things do not always go as planned. This is part of being a maker!
Challenges help us think creatively.

WHAT IS A WEDGE?

What do scissors, airplane wings, and needles have in common? They use wedges! A wedge is like an inclined plane. Both have a sloped side with one raised end. Unlike an inclined plane, a wedge needs a force to lift, stop, or split an object. There are single wedges and double wedges. Double wedges are two wedges joined together with their sloped sides facing out.

SIMPLE MACHINES

A wedge is a **simple machine**. Simple machines are tools with few or no moving parts. We use them to change the amount or direction of a **force**. Force is the **effort** needed to push or pull on an object. A small amount of force on the wide end of a wedge delivers a larger sideways force at the pointed end.

HELP WITH WORK

We call the use of force to move an object from one place to another **work**. Wedges make work easier, faster, or safer in many ways. They often split apart or lift objects. Wedges can also stop objects from moving.

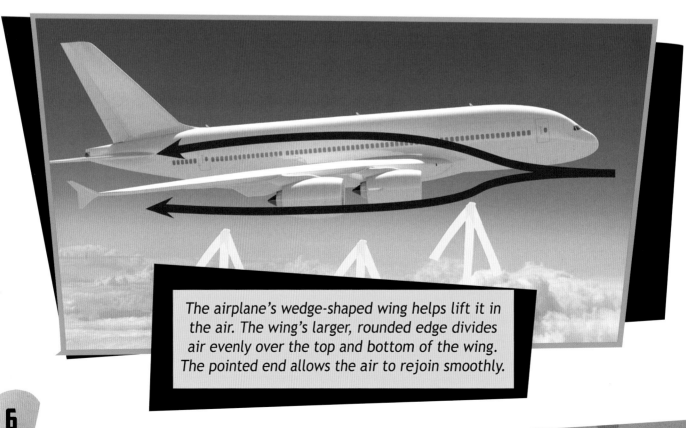

The airplane's wedge-shaped wing helps lift it in the air. The wing's larger, rounded edge divides air evenly over the top and bottom of the wing. The pointed end allows the air to rejoin smoothly.

WEDGES IN ACTION

Unlike **ramps**, wedges only work when force is put on them. Pushing a wedge under a door stops the door from closing, for example. Pushing down on the handle applies force to the wide end of the ax. This force transfers to the sharp, pointed edge that splits the wood.

An ax is a double wedge. Applying a downward force to the wide end of the ax transfers to a sideways force as the pointed edge splits the wood.

MAKE A WEDGE

Making single and double wedges will help you understand the function, or use, of each type of wedge. You will discover how force is applied to wedges and how their different features determine their purpose—whether they stop an object, lift it, or split the object apart. This will help you with the maker missions in this book.

SET IT UP!

1. Cut three rectangles of different sizes out of cardboard. Rectangle **A** is 6 inches (15 cm) by 2.4 inches (6 cm). Rectangle **B** is 6 inches (15 cm) by 6.3 inches (16 cm). Rectangle **C** is 6 inches (15 cm) by 6.7 inches (17 cm).

Materials
- Cardboard
- Scissors
- Masking tape , duct tape, or sticky tack

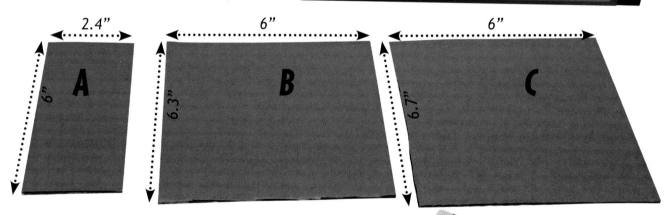

2.4"   A   6"

6"   B   6.3"

6"   C   6.7"

2. Using tape or sticky tack, secure the edges together to form a right-angle triangle. Rectangle A and Rectangle B should form a right angle. Rectangle C forms the sloped side.

> This is a single wedge. When force is applied to the wide end, it transfers, or moves, to the pointed edge which stops or lifts objects.

force

90°

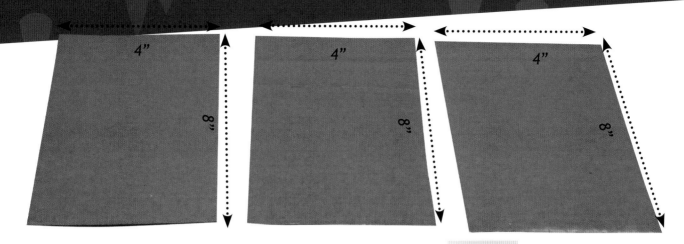

3. Cut three rectangles of the same size out of cardboard. The rectangles should be about 4 inches (10 cm) by 8 inches (20 cm).

4. Using tape or sticky tack, secure the edges of the pieces of cardbard together to form a triangle.

This is a double wedge. The arrows show you the two sloped sides facing out. When force is applied to the wide end, it transfers to the pointed edge which can split objects apart.

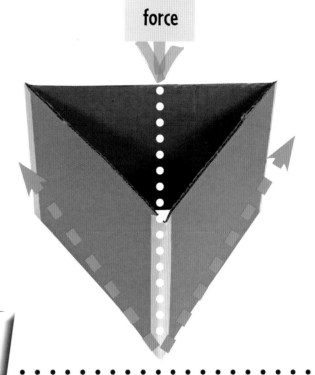

force

Think About It

Try using your wedges to stop, lift, and split apart objects. For example, stop a door from closing, lift a box, and split apart two books placed side by side. How do they compare? Which wedge worked better for each function? Can wedges work if no force is applied to their wide end?

Once you understand how a simple machine works, you will be able to modify, or change, it to solve different problems. How you build each wedge will change based on the criteria of each maker mission. For example, the materials, size, or purpose of the wedge may change from challenge to challenge. Check out the "Modify Your Machine" boxes throughout the book.

Get ready to be creative with wedges! When you begin each of the maker projects in this book, brainstorm **different ideas and solutions.** You may need to modify your simple machine or think outside the box. Write down as many ideas as possible in five minutes. If you're working with other makers, remember to respect their ideas!

When you have decided on an idea, start by making a plan. You should measure each part of your project carefully and make sketches of how it will look. Planning is an important part of being a maker…but remember to also be open-minded. Your project might change as you go. There are endless possibilities!

Helpful hints

Running into problems is part of the maker process. If you are stuck, try some of the following tips:

- Think about problem-solving tools around you. **Ask:** Is there something out there that solves a similar problem?

- Delete or Double Up! **Ask:** What would happen if we removed this part? What would happen if we added another of the same part?

- **Ask:** What would happen if I changed the shape, size, or strength of a material?

- Take a time out! Sometimes, taking a short break can refresh your mind and help you come back ready to work.

- Think about solutions to problems or challenges you have solved in the past. There may be some parts you could add to or change to help you solve this problem or challenge.

WEDGES THAT STOP

Many wedges work a lot like doorstops. They make it easier to stop an object from moving and use only a small amount of force. Devices called wheel chocks, for example, keep large, wheeled objects such as cars from rolling away.

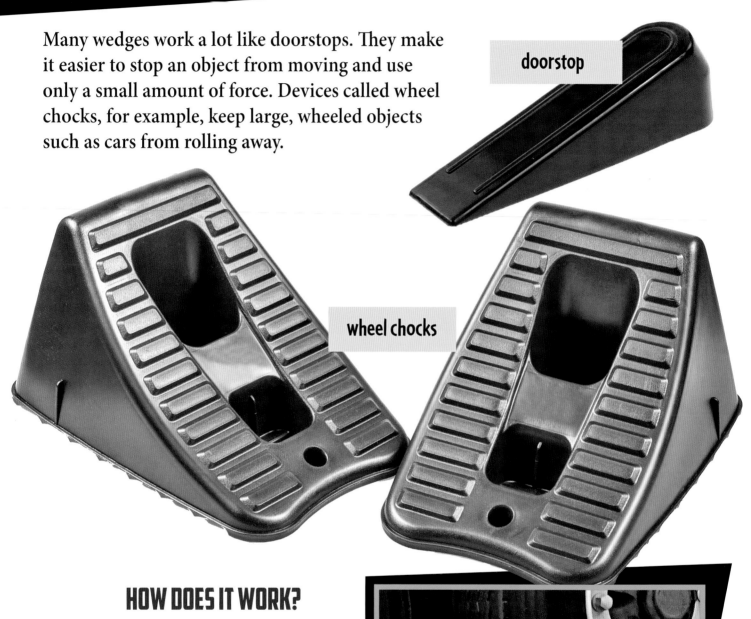

doorstop

wheel chocks

HOW DOES IT WORK?

The thin edge of the wedged wheel chock slides as far as it can go under a wheel. Force is put on the wide edge of the wedge to slide it further under the wheel. This can be as simple as kicking the wheel chock. The wheel presses against the wedge, which in turn presses tightly against the ground. This stops the wheel from rolling.

PUT A STOP TO IT

Wheel chocks do more than make it easy to hold something in place. Keeping wheels from rolling can also improve safety. Picture a grocery cart rolling out of control in a parking lot! When a wheeled object is on sloped ground, force pulls it downhill. Wheel chocks can even keep large objects like airplanes in place.

Larger objects, such as airplanes, use multiple wheel chocks.

TRY IT!

Are you ready to make your own wheel chock? Remember that makers start by planning their projects. This includes brainstorming and drawing your ideas. Flip to page 14 to get started!

MAKE IT STAY

MAKER MISSION

Get ready to make! Create your own wheel chock and then put it to the test. Your wedge must keep a wheeled object from rolling down a sloped surface.

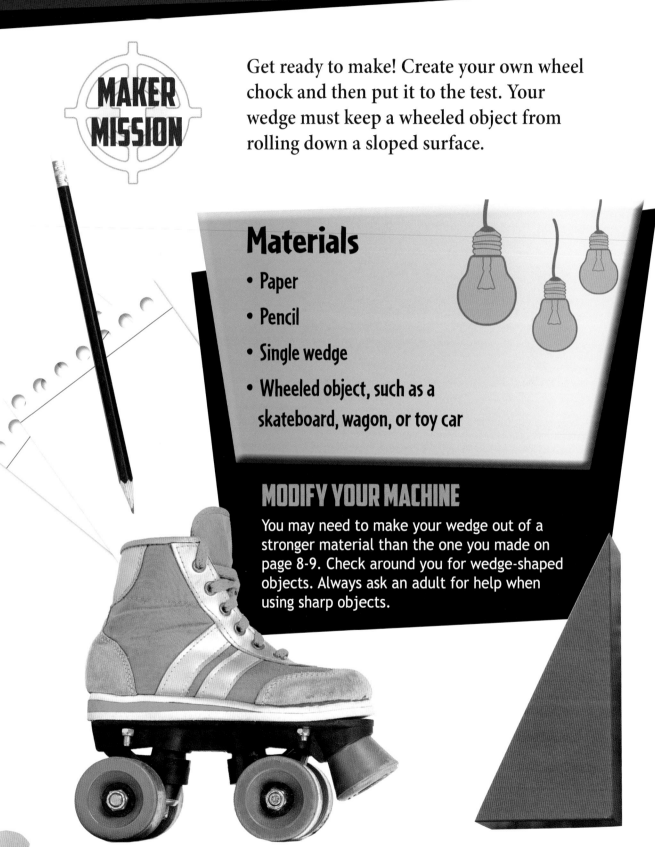

Materials

- Paper
- Pencil
- Single wedge
- Wheeled object, such as a skateboard, wagon, or toy car

MODIFY YOUR MACHINE

You may need to make your wedge out of a stronger material than the one you made on page 8-9. Check around you for wedge-shaped objects. Always ask an adult for help when using sharp objects.

THINK ABOUT IT

Size

How will the size of the wheels on your object affect the size of the wedge that you make?

Design

Materials

How does the surface of the test area affect the materials you use?

Where will you test your creation?

Would using multiple chocks help with this challenge?

How does the wedge's sloped surface affect how you build your wheel chock?

MISSION ACCOMPLISHED

Test your wheel chock on ground that is sloped enough that your wheeled object will roll down it. Did your wedge hold the object in place? If not, what could you try next?

Once your wheel chock works well, go to page 30 to find ideas to rework it.

WEDGES THAT PUSH APART

Wedges can do more than push up against an object—they can go right through them! Wedges with sharp ends make it easier to split or push things apart.

CUTTING WEDGES

Grab a pair of scissors and look at the blades. The blades are double wedges that work together to cut. A single wedge, such as a knife, can also split an object. Wedges can even cut into the ground! The blade on a plow used in a farmer's field is a double wedge. It makes it easier to cut into the soil when planting seeds.

HOW DOES IT WORK?

Remember, a wedge only works when a force is applied to the wide end. Without some sort of effort, the pointed edge cannot split or push apart objects. For example, plow blades attach to handles that a person can push or a horse can pull. This kind of wedge can also be on a frame that connects to a tractor.

TRY IT!

To see how wedges can split objects, make your own and try it. Flip to the next page to get started on the Make it Split challenge. Be creative with your materials and design!

A shovel is another example of a double wedge that cuts into the ground.

MAKE IT SPLIT

Put a wedge to work! Make a wedge that can split or push apart an object. To make this project more challenging, choose a test object that you cannot pull apart with your hands.

Materials

- Paper

- Pencil

- Single or double wedge (Try hunting for solid wedge-shaped objects around your home!)

- Test object for splitting, such as a bar of soap, an apple, or a potato

MODIFY YOUR MACHINE

The thin edge of your wedge will need to be as pointy as possible. Make sure an adult is close by when you build and test it!

THINK ABOUT IT

Materials

Look for wedge-shaped objects that you could repurpose for this project.

Design

How will you make the pointed edge of your wedge sharp enough to split the object?

Size

Will you choose a short, thick wedge or a long, skinny wedge?

How will you put force on the wide end of the wedge?

Which direction will you move the wedge?

MISSION ACCOMPLISHED

Did your wedge make the cut? If not, what could you try next?

Once your wedge works, check out Endless Ideas on page 30 for ways to make it even better.

WEDGES THAT LIFT

A kitchen is a great place to spot wedges making work easier. Imagine that you are cooking pancakes in a hot frying pan. How would you flip them or move them onto a plate? Using your fingers would be tricky to do—and dangerous. You need a wedge!

A HELPING HAND

Some wedges lift loads more easily, quickly, and safely than using your hands. A flipper would help with your pancakes. Using this kind of wedge is similar to using a shovel. The pointed end slides under the pancake, which rests on the wedge's sloped side, or surface.

HOW DOES IT WORK?

The sloped surface of the wedge is important for lifting loads. A load only lifts as high as the height of the sloped surface. What would happen if your pancake flipper had a short, **steep** sloped surface? It would rise up too quickly and the pancake might fall off!

TRY IT!

It is time to put a wedge to work for you. Get some friends together for the next challenge and share your ideas! Remember, teamwork can help you look at your project in different ways. Flip to the next page to get started.

Wedges that lift do not need handles, but they can be helpful for adding force.

MAKE IT LIFT

MAKER MISSION

Create a way to help you do chores quickly and easily—use a wedge to make your bed! Your wedge must lift one edge of the mattress enough to tuck a bedsheet under it.

Materials

- Paper
- Pencil
- Wedge
- Measuring tape or ruler
- Mattress
- Bedsheet

MODIFY YOUR MACHINE

Your wedge needs to be strong enough so that the weight of the mattress will not crush it! Choose a solid material. You also need to make sure the sloped surface of the wedge can lift your mattress high enough.

THINK ABOUT IT

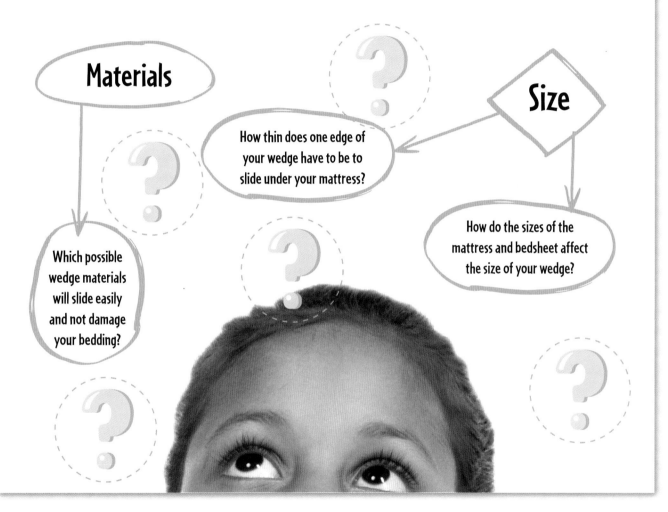

Materials

Size

How thin does one edge of your wedge have to be to slide under your mattress?

Which possible wedge materials will slide easily and not damage your bedding?

How do the sizes of the mattress and bedsheet affect the size of your wedge?

MISSION ACCOMPLISHED

It's time to test your bed-making wedge! If it does not work as you planned, what could you try next?

Once you succeed at this challenge, go to page 30 for more ideas.

WEDGES THAT PART WATER

You have read about wedges that stop, split, and lift. It is amazing what this simple machine with no moving parts can do! Adding wedges to other machines creates even more ways to make work easier, faster, and safer. To learn more about simple machines that work together, flip to page 28.

WET WEDGES!

Wedges are an important part of many machines. For example, most boats have a double wedge-shaped **bow**. The bow is the front of a boat. A wedge parts water along the length of a boat. This helps it move quickly and easily through water using less effort.

HOW DOES IT WORK?

With boats, the thin edge of the wedge is the first part to move through water. The long, thin wedges on canoes and other boats part the water smoothly over a longer distance. Motorboats with a shorter, wider wedge at the bow part the water quickly. Their wedge shape creates more waves.

TRY IT!

Build your own toy boat to see a wedge-shaped bow in action. Remember that makers always stick to it—even when projects aren't easy. Flip the page to get started!

MAKE A BOAT

MAKER MISSION

Get your wedge into the water! Make a boat that has a wedge-shaped bow. Your boat must float and move forward in the water when pushed.

Materials

- Paper
- Pencil
- Double wedge that floats
- Plastic knife or craft knife (ask an adult to use the knife for you when cutting material)
- Test basin filled with water, such as a sink, bathtub, or pool

MODIFY YOUR MACHINE

You will need to make your wedge using a waterproof material that floats and is easy to shape, such as Styrofoam.

THINK ABOUT IT

Size

How does the size of your wedge material, or your test area, place limits on your project?

How will you plan for those limits?

Design

How will drawing your ideas before you start help you?

What other ways could you make your boat move forward?

What other elements can you add to your boat to make it fun to use?

MISSION ACCOMPLISHED

Test your boat in water. Does it float and move forward when pushed? Make notes about anything that you need to change. Keep testing and changing your design until it works well.

Try something new with the ideas on page 30.

MORE MACHINES

There are five other kinds of simple machines.
Check them out in the chart below!

NAME	PURPOSE	PICTURE	EXAMPLES
inclined planes	move objects between two heights		water slide funnel wheelchair ramp
levers	move, lift, or lower objects	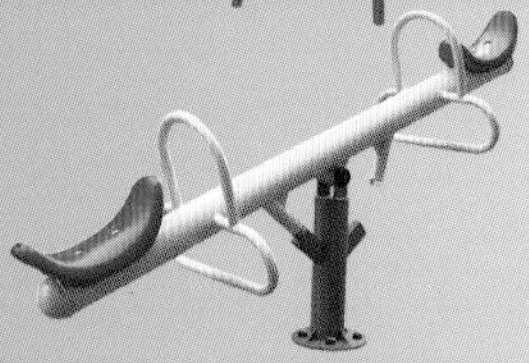	seesaw balancing scale catapult
pulleys	lift, lower, or move objects; transfer force from one object to another		flagpole zip line bicycle chain
screws	join, cut into, lift, or lower objects		jar and lid drill light bulb
wheels and axles	move objects		Ferris wheel rolling pin skateboard

COMPLEX MACHINES

Joining two or more simple machines creates a complex machine. Believe it or not, a pizza cutter is a **complex machine**! Its blade is a very thin wedge. The round blade is also a wheel that turns on an axle. The attached handle is a lever.

CHANGE IT UP!

How could you use a wedge and another simple machine to make a complex machine? Start by experimenting with one of the projects from this book. Flip to page 30 for more project inspiration.

ENDLESS IDEAS

Makers are always learning and coming up with new ideas! You could make each of the projects in this book in many different ways. For example:

Make It Stay (pages 14-15):

• How could you add sides to your wheel chock to help it stop and support a bicycle wheel so it does not tip over? Research levers to get some ideas.

Make It Split (pages 18-19):

• How could you modify your wedge to use it to carve the object? Be careful with sharp wedges! Always make sure an adult is present.

• What would happen if you added some kind of handle?

Make It Lift (pages 22-23):

• If you are working with a team, how could you use multiple wedges to make a bed even faster?

• What other ways could you use a wedge to help you with a chore? (Hint: Do you have a messy bedroom floor? Remember that shovels are wedges!)

Make a Boat (pages 26-27):

• Which other waterproof, floating materials could you use to make a boat?

• How could making the bow of your boat narrower or wider affect your project?

LEARNING MORE

BOOKS

Bailey, Gerry. *Splitting Apart: The Wedge.* Crabtree, 2014.

Christiansen, Jennifer. *Get to Know Wedges.* Crabtree, 2009.

Feldmann, Roseann. *How Do Simple Machines Work: Put Wedges to the Test.* Lerner, 2011.

Tomljanovic, Tatiana. *Wedges.* Weigl, 2013.

● ●

WEBSITES

Watch a short video about wedges and other simple machines at the PBS website.
http://bit.ly/2fMyzqI

Review basic facts about wedges at this website.
http://easyscienceforkids.com/a-wedge/

Visit this page to find out more about how wedges and other simple machines join to make boats.
www.lcmm.org/education/resource/maritime-machines.html

● ●

GLOSSARY

bow The front end of a boat

brainstorm To come up with as many ideas as possible to solve a problem or answer a question

complex machine A machine that combines at least two simple machines

effort The amount of energy, or power, used to do something

force The effort needed to push or pull on an object

inclined plane A sloping surface with one raised end

makerspace A place where makers work together and share their ideas and resources

ramp An incline plane with a flat surface

simple machine A tool with few or no moving parts that people use to change the amount or direction of a force

steep Describes a sloped surface that has a sharp angle

wedge A simple machine made of one or two sloped sides

work The use of force to move an object from one place to another

INDEX

ABOUT THE AUTHORS

Tim Miller is a mechanical engineer who loves to work with his hands. He is also a founding board member of Fusion Labworks, a maker community. Rebecca Sjonger is the author of over 40 children's books, including three titles in the *Be a Maker!* series.